To

Tracy Vincent

and

Rodney Vincent

With best wishes,

from

Aunt Faye

DON'T RIDE THE BUS ON MONDAY

THE ROSA PARKS STORY

by

Louise Meriwether

illustrated by David Scott Brown

PRENTICE-HALL, Inc., Englewood Cliffs, N.J.

DON'T RIDE THE BUS ON MONDAY *The Rosa Parks Story*
by Louise Meriwether

Printed in the United States of America
10   9   8   7   6   5   4   3   2

Prentice-Hall International, Inc., London
Prentice-Hall of Australia, Pty. Ltd., North Sydney
Prentice-Hall of Canada, Ltd., Toronto
Prentice-Hall of India Private Ltd., New Delhi
Prentice-Hall of Japan, Inc., Tokyo

Library of Congress Cataloging in Publication Data

Meriwether, Louise.
   Don't ride the bus on Monday.

   SUMMARY: A brief biography of the Alabama black
woman whose refusal to give up her seat on the bus
marked the beginning of the civil rights movement.

   1.   Parks, Rosa, 1913–   —Juvenile literature.
2.   Segregation in transportation—Montgomery, Ala.—
Juvenile literature.   3.   Montgomery, Ala.—Race question
—Juvenile literature.   [1.   Parks, Rosa, 1913–
2.   Negros—Biography.   3.   Negroes—Civil rights]
I.   Brown, David, 1926–   illus.   II.   Title.
E185.97.P3M4   323.4'092'4 [B] [92]   72–6331
ISBN   0–13–218759–7

To Aunt Helen and Uncle Mac, with love

Seven-year-old Rosa was so excited she bounced as she walked. She tugged on her mother's hand, hurrying her down the dirt road. Then she waved to her grandparents and her brother, who were standing in the doorway of their raggedy farmhouse. They waved back. Rosa skipped alongside of her mother on this wonderful, wonderful day. It was her first day of school in Pine Level, Alabama.

Rosa and Mother came to the fork in the road. There was the lovely new school building. White children played in the yard. Rosa and Mother kept on walking. They walked and walked. At last they came to the colored schoolhouse near the edge of town. It was a tottering, one-room shack.

Mother took Rosa inside and left her there. The black teacher smiled and pointed to a bench crowded with youngsters.

Rosa sat down. She could already read. Mother had taught her. And she had been so eager to come to school and learn more. But this school had no desks, no windows, no pretty picture books. Rosa was so disappointed she almost cried.

As the days passed her disappointment faded. Rosa liked her teacher and her lessons and playing with her new friends. But every day she had to pass the school for white children. And every day she wondered, Why do they have a nice new school while black children have a shack?

Rosa had been born in Tuskegee, Alabama, on February 4, 1913. Her father was James McCauley, a house builder. Her mother, Leona McCauley, was a teacher. Rosa's parents were separated now and her father lived up North.

Rosa lived on a farm with her mother, her grandparents and her brother, Sylvester. He was only four and it was Rosa's job to take care of him.

The family raised barely enough food on the farm to feed themselves. They were very poor. Teaching jobs were scarce and when Mother couldn't find one she sewed for her black neighbors. She was also a hairdresser.

Rosa's grandparents were Sylvester and Rosa Edwards. To earn money they picked crops on nearby plantations. So did Rosa. Her school closed three months earlier than the white school so black children could work in the fields. Rosa gathered corn and peanuts and sweet potatoes right next to her grandparents.

Grandpa and Grandma both had been slaves. In the evenings Grandpa told Rosa and Sylvester stories about his childhood. He told them how once an overseer had beaten him so badly that he still limped.

Grandpa said Alabama was still a dangerous place for black people. At times white men with sheets over their heads rode through town on horseback. They burned down black churches and farms trying to keep black folks in "their place."

Their place was to step off the sidewalks to let white people pass. They had to stand aside in stores while whites were served first. Black people did the most backbreaking work for the smallest pay.

If black people refused to do these things they could be jailed. Or beaten. Or killed. Grandpa did not believe though that black people had to stay in "their place." He always kept his shotgun nearby to protect his family.

Often Rosa was so frightened she could not sleep at night. She lay in bed dreaming of going North. She heard that black people were treated better there. So many relatives and friends were leaving Alabama. Rosa wanted to leave also.

When Rosa was eleven, Mother saved up enough money to send her to a private school in Montgomery, Alabama. Montgomery was a big city, and Rosa lived there with Mother's sister and her five children.

At the new school all the teachers were white. The students were all black. In addition to their regular studies they also learned sewing, cooking, rug making and basket weaving.

One day during class the teacher said that Africans were savages. She said, "You children are lucky your ancestors were brought to this country as slaves so you could be civilized."

Rosa did not feel lucky. It made her sad to think she had come from a race of savages. Later, when Rosa was older, she learned the truth. Africans were civilized hundreds of years before they had been brought to America as slaves. They had built great cities and universities in Africa.

When Rosa was in high school, Mother became ill. Rosa quit school and found a servant's job. Then she met Raymond Parks, a barber, and they were married the next year. Now Rosa Parks was able to return to high school and graduate.

After graduation, jobs were hard to find and Rosa had to work wherever she could. She did housecleaning. She sewed at home. She worked for a black insurance company and was also a clerk in an office.

In 1943 Rosa Parks joined the National Association for the Advancement of Colored People, often called the NAACP. The NAACP fought for the rights of black people. Mr. E. E. Nixon was the head of the NAACP in Montgomery. He and Mrs. Parks worked together to help black people vote.

Black people as citizens had the right to vote. But in the South many tactics were used to keep them from voting. They were given unfair tests, and if they failed they could not vote. Often they were fired from their jobs for trying to vote. Sometimes they were beaten up and thrown in jail.

Mrs. Parks and Mr. Nixon were both warned they would be hurt if they continued to encourage and help other blacks. But they kept on with their efforts, and in time many more black people were able to vote.

ISTRAR

During this time Mrs. Parks also had a regular job. She was now a tailor's helper in a downtown department store.

Often she walked home from work because she hated to ride the bus. Black people had to sit in the back of the bus. They had to give up their seats to whites if the bus became crowded. Some drivers even made black people enter the bus through the back door. Mrs. Parks refused to do this, and she often got into arguments with the bus drivers.

On December 1, 1955, Mrs. Parks was very tired. Her work had been especially hard that day, and she took the bus home. She sat in the back in the first row of the colored section. Soon all the seats up front were filled. White people were standing.

The bus driver said, "You Negroes in the first row get up so white folks can sit down."

The man next to Mrs. Parks stood up. But Mrs. Parks was so weary her bones felt as if they were melting. She asked the driver, "Why should I give up my seat to a white man? I paid the same fare he did."

The driver became angry. He yelled at Mrs. Parks to stand up. Then he rushed from the bus and returned with two policemen. Still Mrs. Parks refused to move.

The police arrested her. They put her in their police car and took her to jail, where she was placed in a cell. Later that night Mr. Nixon and a white lawyer secured her release from jail.

Black people were angry at the arrest of Mrs. Parks. Mr. Nixon called together several ministers and a big meeting was held at Dexter Avenue Baptist Church. Dr. Martin Luther King was the new minister there.

Every seat in the church was filled. Crowds outside were still trying to get in when Mrs. Parks was introduced. She stood up and told about her arrest.

The people grew angrier. Riding in the back of the bus had made them all feel like dirt. Now they decided to protest to the bus owners. They wanted courteous treatment from the bus drivers. They wanted to be able to keep their seats. To prove they were serious, they decided not to ride the buses on Monday.

The meeting broke up and the people left to spread the word to the others. "Don't ride the bus on Monday. Walk."

Ministers preached this message from their pulpits. Children passed out leaflets.

On Monday morning Mrs. Parks walked to work. The roads were jammed with black folks tramping to their jobs. The buses rolled by almost empty.

The bus owners refused to listen to the demands of the people. More meetings were held. The people decided: "We will keep on walking." Dr. King was chosen as the leader of this protest.

Walking to work every day was especially hard on the women. Many of them worked long hours for white families. They were the cleaning women, the cooks, the washerwomen, the children's nurses. Some women had to get up at three in the morning and walk twelve miles to and from work.

The NAACP took the matter to the highest law of the land, the Supreme Court. They asked the court to change the local laws that forced black people to ride in the back of the bus. Many months passed before the court made its decision.

And the people in Montgomery, Alabama, kept on walking. Mrs. Parks lost her job. The barber shop fired her husband. The churches raised money and bought private cars and station wagons. Now Mrs. Parks worked in an office setting up rides for the workers. Still there were not enough rides for all the people. They kept on walking.

The town officials tried to force black people to ride the buses. Mrs. Parks was arrested again. So was Dr. King and more than a hundred others. Dr. King's house was bombed. When Mr. Nixon's life was threatened, he sat up all night on his porch cradling his shotgun. Mrs. Parks received telephone calls and letters threatening to kill her. Still the people kept on walking.

Mrs. Parks traveled to other cities. She talked at meetings about the bus boycott. What had started as a one-day protest lasted for 381 days. The bus company lost thousands of dollars.

Finally, the Supreme Court had its say. It ruled that black people could sit anywhere on buses and trains throughout the South. Never again would they have to give up their seats to whites. The black people had won.

From this success in Montgomery, Alabama, Dr. King went on to become a powerful leader. And Mrs. Parks at last said good-bye to Alabama. She and her husband and mother moved to Detroit where her brother now lived.

In speaking about herself Mrs. Parks says: "I'm just an average citizen. Many black people before me were arrested for defying the bus laws. They prepared the way."

Many heroic black people did prepare the way for Mrs. Parks. But her courage in refusing to give up her seat on the bus led to a nationwide revolt. Black people began to demand *freedom now*. Not tomorrow but today. That demand is still being heard throughout the land and could lead to a better America.